Rugby

Rita Storey

FRANKLIN WATTS
LONDON • SYDNEY

First published in 2009 by
Franklin Watts
338 Euston Road
London NW1 3BH

Franklin Watts Australia
Level 17/207 Kent Street
Sydney NSW 2000

Series editor: Sarah Peutrill
Art director: Jonathan Hair

Series designed and created for Franklin Watts by Storeybooks.
Designer: Rita Storey
Editor: Nicola Edwards
Photography: Tudor Photography, Banbury (unless otherwise stated)

Picture credits
© Jack Sullivan/Alamy p6; David Rogers/Getty Images p26 and 27;
i-stock p23.

Thanks to Matt Davies of the Saracens Academy, Oaklands College,
for all his help. Also thanks to Jackson, Jake, Jamie and Sam for their
participation in the book.

A CIP catalogue record for this book is available from the British
Library.

Dewey classification: 796.333
ISBN: 978 0 7496 8500 3

Printed in China

Franklin Watts is a division of Hachette
Children's Books, an Hachette UK company.
www.hachette.co.uk

Words in **bold** are
in the glossary on
page 30.

Contents

Meet the players

Rugby is a fast, tough outdoor sport played by two teams of 15 players. The object of the game is to score as many points as possible and to stop the opposing team from scoring. Points are gained by scoring a **try**, a **conversion**, a **penalty** or a **drop goal**.

Most people play rugby at school or for a local club for enjoyment and to keep fit, but for some talented players rugby will also become their career. In this book you will meet four rugby players who are aiming to play rugby professionally. They will share their experiences with you of the talent, training and dedication it takes to make that happen.

Jake Sharp

*I am 17 years of age. I am a **back** and play at number ten. I started to learn to play rugby at the age of seven at Saracens amateurs, where I played in the first team up to under-16s. I also played for my school, Sheredes. At secondary school I represented my county from 14 to 16, and during the under-16 season I was lucky enough to represent London division. From there I earned my place in the England under 16-side, where I gained two **caps**. I am currently in the England under-18 Conference Squad.*

The thing about rugby that wanted to make me compete was the love of the game, the banter and friendship within the squad, the different characters and the ability to be in a team that could create a winning environment.

Sam Stanley

I am 16 years old. I am a back and play number 12 or 13. I started playing rugby at the age of four. I have played for my school, for my local club, Thurrock, and for Essex county.

My main hobby is playing rugby. Other than that, I like to play a bit of guitar and also meet up with friends.

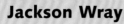

Jackson Wray

I am 17 years old. I am a forward and my position is number eight. I began playing rugby at the age of 14 for my local club, Westcliff RFC, and my secondary school, King John School, Thundersley. At 15 I began playing county rugby, where I represented Essex.

Originally I enjoyed playing rugby as most of my friends had played the game since they were young. Outside rugby, I like to play golf and squash and listen to music.

Jamie Bache

I am 17 and I am a forward playing at number seven. I started playing rugby when I was six years old. As I grew up, I played for my school, then for Burnham–on–Crouch rugby club and eventually for Essex county.

The enjoyment I get from rugby is completely different to any other sport, it challenges you and you get to battle against your opposite number. Outside rugby, I enjoy socialising with friends.

These four players have played in the England under-16s squad and are hoping to compete at the highest level.

Starting out

What motivates rugby players to take up the sport? It may be encouragement from school or a local club or it may be having other family members who play.

I've wanted to be a rugby player ever since I understood what I was doing. My family are pretty much a rugby family. My uncle Joe played for New Zealand in 1987 when they won the Rugby World Cup. I hope that making it that far is in the family.

Mini rugby

There are several ways to start playing rugby. Most rugby clubs have a mini rugby section for both boys and girls from the second year of primary school. Girls and boys play in mixed teams up to the age of 12. Players who want to continue after that age go on to play junior or youth rugby. Colts rugby is played by older teenagers and is the stage between junior rugby and the full adult game.

A non-contact version of rugby is played in schools. It is called tag rugby. In tag rugby the players have a ribbon attached by velcro to their belt or shorts. Instead of a **tackle** by another player the ribbon (or tag) is pulled off.

Touch rugby is a simpler version of the full game. Players do not tackle their opponents, but instead touch them using their hands or the ball. It is ideal for beginners, although people of all abilities can play. Touch rugby is very popular in Australia and New Zealand.

Academies

Rugby players with the talent and dedication to compete at a high level may be accepted at a sports academy. The four rugby players featured in this book are at Oaklands College in St Albans, which runs the Saracens Academy in

Young players compete in a tag rugby match.

Rugby sevens
Rugby sevens has almost the same rules as rugby union and is played on the same pitches. The major differences are that the games are shorter and there are only seven players on each team instead of 15.

Players at the Saracens Academy train very hard to achieve a high level of strength and fitness.

partnership with Saracens, a Premiership rugby club. The college's partnership with Saracens allows the players to train every day as well as continuing their academic studies and playing for the college team.

*When I was young, I remember going on for a few weeks about wanting to take part in some sort of sport. My dad was a keen rugby player who thought that it would be the right way for me to go. I picked up rugby very quickly and had good **hand-eye co-ordination** and evasion skills. The first ever game I played in was at the Saracens Amateurs festival. I hadn't trained, but they were short on numbers. I remember just running round like a headless chicken. I didn't decide that I wanted to make rugby my career until I was about 15; that was when I realised I had the potential to be good.*

My dad, my uncle and my granddad all encouraged me when I first started to play rugby. My uncle played rugby for the USA and American football for the New England Patriots.

When I realised you could get paid for playing, I decided that I wanted rugby to be my career.

Originally I didn't improve at any great pace, I was just playing the game because I enjoyed it. I think that I improved mainly because of the enjoyment and also the desire to win. A year into playing for my school and club, I had a slight inkling that I could be a good player. When I realised that I was one of the best players in my school – that was the biggest moment.

The coach

Good coaching is vital in a rugby player's career. A coach's ability to spot talent in a young player is the first step in a long and complex relationship.

The role of a coach

Coaches are involved in every aspect of a player's development. There may be specialists, such as a strength and fitness coach and a dietician working with the players, but their coach has an overview of how everything is progressing. It is the coach's job to develop an individual training programme and continually assess a player's development. The coach is also there to motivate and support the players. The aim is to build players up to maximum fitness in preparation for important games. In addition, players and their coach work constantly to achieve new goals and levels of excellence.

Meet the coach: Matt Davies

I am 28. I went to De Montfort University, Bedford and played for Bedford Blues. I became the Rugby Football Union Development Officer for Essex in 2003. In 2006 I became Academy Coach at Saracens, running the RFU Saracens AASE (Advanced Apprenticeship in Sporting Excellence) scheme in conjunction with Oaklands College.

Our coach gives us both positive and negative information on our games and training so we can improve on whatever we need to. We usually go through video analysis so we can see what we have done both right and wrong. We also analyse ourselves on paper.

Jamie and Sam work on a training drill under the watchful eye of their coach.

Being able to watch video recordings of matches to analyse them is a useful training tool.

Analysis

The coach helps individual players to analyse their performance and identify their strengths and weaknesses. One of the ways in which a coach does this is by playing back video recordings of matches and looking at aspects of a player's performance. Matt shows his players video footage of matches so that they can see where things went wrong (or right). The players also fill in match analysis forms after a game and discuss them with the coach.

Coach's notes: analysis

After a match, always analyse your performance. Look at your:
• preparation for the game
• targets in the game
• performance in the game.

Also think about your:
• physical performance
• tactical performance
• skill level
• mental attitude.

Motivation

Players have regular one-to-one meetings with their coach so that he can identify short-, medium- and long-term goals. The object is to create players who not only want to play well for themselves but also for their team and their club.

*I have different coaches for each area of the game. There are three skills coaches and a strength and conditioning coach. All of my coaches have helped me improve through persistent work on all areas of my game and also by mentoring me in terms of my organisation and **nutrition**.*

9

Strength and conditioning

As well as training for the position in which they play, all rugby players need a high level of general fitness. They need to be able to perform at their best for the whole 80 minutes of a match. Being fit will also help them to avoid getting injured.

Every week I do five or six strength and conditioning sessions at the club's gym. Our strength and conditioning coach, Andy Edwards, monitors our progress through the year and adapts our training to fit our targets.

Strength and conditioning coach

Individual players have a programme designed for them by a strength and conditioning coach. The players do these exercises in the academy's gym. Each programme takes into account the positions in which the individuals play, as well as the stage they are at in the season. The number of strength and conditioning sessions increases before the match season starts. During **pre-season** the players increase the number to five **cardiovascular** sessions and five strength sessions a week.

Types of exercise

All the players do a range of cardiovascular exercises. These exercises are designed to increase the heart rate and strengthen the heart and lungs. This means that players can use more oxygen and exercise more intensively without getting out of breath. It also increases their tolerance to **lactic acid** and **adrenaline**. These

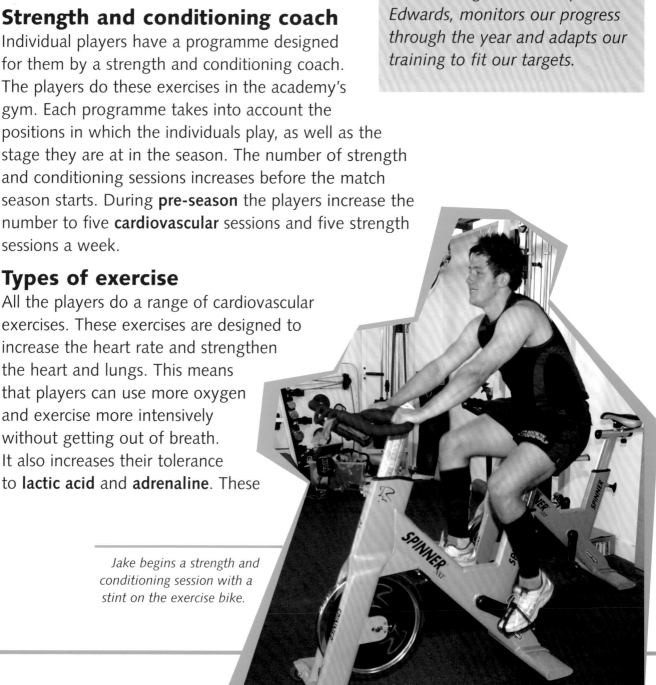

Jake begins a strength and conditioning session with a stint on the exercise bike.

Jackson needs to have powerful arms and shoulders. Here he climbs a rope using his arms to support his body weight.

Sam jumps from a standing start onto a table.

chemicals build up in the bloodstream and cause pain in the muscles when someone exercises very hard. The players also do strength exercises that are designed to build muscle. Power exercises help them to access an explosive burst of speed when they need it.

Coach's notes: training

Physical preparation is important, as strength, speed and power are essential characteristics in modern elite rugby players. A professional strength and conditioning coach can help you achieve your maximum fitness levels. Incorrect training can lead to injuries.

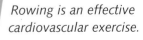

Rowing is an effective cardiovascular exercise.

In training

For these academy rugby players training starts at 7.45am when the players meet for breakfast. They train almost every day. Training sessions are taken by one of the academy's coaches. Training on the pitch allows players to practise all the skills they will need to use in a match.

The players start a training session with a jog around the pitch to warm up.

The warm-up

Before training or competing, rugby players do a series of stretches to loosen up their muscles. They also do cardiovascular exercises. These exercises are designed to increase their heart rate so that they are ready to perform at a high level.

Training times will all depend on the time of season and what is coming up. For example, over the pre-season stage of the year, we would be in at 8.30am and wouldn't finish till 5pm.

Leg swings loosen up the leg muscles ready for training. This reduces the risk of leg injuries.

Sam uses speed and footwork to beat a defender.

Tactics

The players learn about tactics in the classroom and their training sessions are where they put what they have learned into practice. They learn passing moves for both defence and attack, which they can use to gain an advantage over the other team. Players work on these moves over and over in practice drills.

Beating your opponent

Coaches say that if players cannot out-run their opponents, they must out-wit them instead. Players practise **dummies**, **swerves** and **sidesteps** to confuse the opposition and keep the ball.

Training all the time also gives me confidence on the rugby pitch.

I enjoy training most of the time, but not when I feel unfit or I make mistakes. I most enjoy training that is based on the needs of the position in which I play.

13

Training for forwards

All the players in a rugby team need different skills for the position in which they play. Each position in the team has a series of responsibilities that goes with it. Positions one to eight are the forwards in the team.

What the forwards do

The forwards are responsible for getting **possession** of the ball and keeping it. They are usually the tallest and most powerful players in the team.

A few times a month I meet with the other forwards in the back row to train specifically for our position. The Saracens' forwards coach, Alex Sanderson, often leads the sessions, which are a great help to me.

Jackson plays at number eight, a position which is in the back row of the forwards in the **scrum** and is a link between the forwards and the backs. Jamie plays at number seven which is one of the two **flankers** in the team.

The scrum

A scrum is made up of the eight forwards in both teams (the **pack**) who form three lines. The players in the pack lock arms to bind the scrum together. They put their heads down and meet the opposing pack shoulder to shoulder. Each member of the pack has a very specific role in the scrum. The number nine (the **scrum half**) feeds the ball into the scrum and the two packs begin to challenge for possession by trying to kick the ball back to a team-mate.

This piece of gym equipment helps players to develop upper body strength and so increase their power in a scrum.

Flipping a tractor tyre is an exercise designed to increase the power in a player's arms and shoulders.

*My part in the scrum is on the outside, pushing the **prop** in. I have to be ready to break off from the scrum quickly if I get possession of the ball. In the line-out I might be jumping for the ball or supporting the player who jumps, so we practise both in training.*

Lifting a tackle bag simulates the action used by some of the players in a line-out.

If play is stopped by the referee because of a minor **infringement**, such as passing or knocking a ball forward, he may call for a scrum to re-start play. The scrum is one of the most dangerous parts of playing rugby union, particularly for those in the front row who take a lot of the weight. There are many rules and regulations surrounding the scrum, as a scrum that collapses can cause major neck injuries to the players.

The line-out

If a ball is kicked into touch (out of the playing area) it is put back in play with a **line-out**. Up to seven forwards from both teams make a line at right angles to the touchline and a metre apart. A player outside the touchline throws the ball high in the air between the two lines. A player from each team jumps to catch the ball while his team-mates support him in the air. Each team has its own system of signals to let the player throwing in know which of their players will be jumping for the ball.

Training for backs

Players in positions 9 to 15 in a rugby team are called the backs. The backs are mainly responsible for creating and converting point-scoring opportunities once the ball has been won by the forwards. The role of the backs is to move the ball towards their opponents' try line by running and kicking the ball. Backs need to be very agile and have dynamic speed.

Kicking

The backs are responsible for a range of different kicks. They can chip the ball forward and follow it at speed. They can also make a high kick, placing the ball so that when it lands another

As a back, it is vital that you always do extra work on top of normal sessions to guarantee 100% performance all the time. I try and get in at least one passing, one kicking and one tackling session a week. I also try and do as much place kicking as possible because it is a very big weapon within a game. The best way to practise a skill is to get the technique right and then be able to perform it under pressure. That is when you know you have mastered the skill.

Sam and Jake demonstrate a drop kick (left) and a place kick (right).

Dragging this piece of equipment, called a sled, helps players to develop powerful leg muscles.

Sam jumps off the floor with a weighted bar on his shoulders. This exercise helps to develop his leg muscles.

Kicking is one of the key skills that I practise, as it plays a major role for my position in a game.

team member is there to catch it. These kicks, called **drop kicks**, are done by dropping the ball and kicking it as it begins to rise after touching the ground. Drop kicks can also be used to score a drop goal.

Backs can also score points by kicking the ball between the goalposts for penalties and conversions. This is called a **place kick** as the ball is placed on a kicking tee or into a hole in the pitch made with a player's heel.

Jake plays at number ten, which is the position called **fly half**. The fly half, usually the player who takes goal kicks, must practise kicking with both power and accuracy.

Sam plays at number 12 or 13, which are inside and outside **centre** positions. The centres work with the fly half to try to find gaps in the opposition's defensive line. They spend time practising sprinting and kicking in their training sessions.

17

Core skills

The core skills that every player must practise over and over again are passing, catching, running and tackling. These are not skills that players learn once and then know forever - they must be constantly refined throughout a player's career.

The coach will expect a passing drill like this one to be 100% accurate.

Passing

Players must pass the ball backwards or (in a **lateral** pass) to the side. They need to pass accurately and with just the right amount of speed to a team-mate who is in the right place to catch the ball. Passing or throwing the ball forward is not allowed. If a player passes the ball forward on purpose, the referee may award the other team a penalty kick or penalty points. If the ball went forward accidentally, then play may be restarted with a scrum (see page 14).

Catching

Catching is just as important as throwing. If a throw is good but the receiving player drops the ball, the other team may gain possession. Players learn to catch the ball with both hands and pull it into the body as they run with it.

Jackson is practising catching a ball while it is still high in the air.

Tackling

Jackson and Jamie practise tackling.

To tackle is to bring a player who is carrying the ball to the ground. Tackling can be dangerous and there are rules about how it can and cannot be done. Players are not allowed to tackle above shoulder height as this could cause serious injury. Tackling is not about just strength, it is a technique to be practised and perfected.

Running

Jackson running with the ball in practice.

Unless a player is much faster than all the opponents on the pitch, simply running in a straight line is unlikely to be enough to score a try. Players practise using swerves to wrongfoot the opposition. They must also be aware of who is around them and be able to decide quickly whether to pass the ball to a team-mate, kick it or keep running with it.

Our skill coaches use various drills to improve the core areas of the game. In a session, we spend the majority of the time working on core skills with and without defenders. Once we have perfected a drill, the coaches develop the task to make it more difficult (usually by adding defenders for extra pressure).

19

Lifestyle

Learning to balance rugby training, academic work and a social life can be very difficult. There are sacrifices that have to be made, but these players think it is worth it.

*I live on **campus** at college – this makes it quite easy to manage my school work at the same time as training.*

Academic work

Sports academies allow young players to balance their training with their academic studies. The Oaklands Academy Rugby Programme is a full-time course on which players spend half the time improving their rugby skills on the training field, and the rest of the week in lessons. The course offers learners diplomas or certificates in Sport Performance and Excellence. As well as this, students study drug awareness, sports leadership, first aid in sport and nutrition. The students also take their RFU Level 1 Coaching Award and a Sports Leader Award.

My timetable is balanced very well between rugby and my school work. I do my assignments in the evenings after school and I have my leisure time later in the evenings, and at weekends.

Organisation

Joining a sports academy may mean living on campus and being away from home for the first time. The players have to deal with responsibilities such as making sure they eat at the right times and having a clean kit for each session.

Diet

Rugby players burn a lot of calories during training so they do not need to limit the

Players who are part of the academy spend half of their week in the classroom.

amount of food they eat. Forwards in particular need to be very strong and muscular, so they have to increase their calorie intake. This does not mean regular trips to fast food restaurants though, as it is important that the calories they eat are from the right foods. The strength and conditioning coach works out a daily eating plan for players who have target weights to achieve.

My strength and fitness coach has set out a plan of what I must eat during a day. I eat 6,000 calories a day. I complete an online food log so that my coaches can monitor what I eat.

Social life

Dedicating yourself to a sport at a young age can mean missing out on leisure time and seeing friends. Most young players feel that achieving their goals makes up for the sacrifices they have to make. The academy rugby players live on or close to the campus and spend a lot of time training together. Friendships are made through their shared love of rugby.

I have had to drop the other sports I used to participate in – swimming, athletics and football – but it is the price you pay if you want to follow your ambition.

The players drink a protein shake after their training to help rebuild and repair muscles.

There is time for going out with your friends but in training you bond with the other players and it is like a family. We always make time for socials within the group.

Injuries

Injuries are inevitable in rugby as it is a fast, physically demanding contact sport. Some positions in the team are more at risk than others. The backs are less likely to sustain serious injuries than the forwards.

RICE

Many joint and muscle injuries can be sorted out fairly easily with what's known as RICE: rest, ice (keeping the injury cold using ice packs), compression (wrapping the injured area with an elastic bandage) and elevation (raising the injured area above your heart). However, more serious injuries are also common.

In the 2007/2008 season, I had a number of injuries one after the other which put me out of action for long periods of time. Early in the season I suffered two **concussions** *which put me out for six weeks. Also, towards the end of the season, I broke a bone in my eye socket which meant I was out for an extra eight weeks.*

Learning to tackle safely but effectively takes a lot of practice.

Fitness

Being fully fit and prepared for a game can help protect against injuries, particularly muscle strains. The players' gym sessions include exercises which focus on the prevention of injuries.

Follow the rules

Serious injuries can happen when players do not follow the rules. The rules are there to keep rugby as safe as it can be without taking away any of the elements that make it so exciting to play and to watch.

Safe tackling

Tackle injuries are very common. The main rule for safe tackling is to make sure that there is no contact above the shoulders. If this rule is broken, the referee has a choice of actions (see page 25).

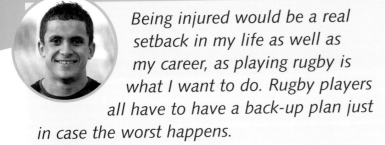

Being injured would be a real setback in my life as well as my career, as playing rugby is what I want to do. Rugby players all have to have a back-up plan just in case the worst happens.

I was out for six weeks once with an ankle injury when I twisted over on it. I also had a collar bone injury when a player landed on me and I was out for two months.

I have had a couple of injuries that have kept me out of training, and in turn missed opportunities due to this. I recently had concussion and missed three weeks of training and games. A year ago, I broke my thumb and was out for six weeks. I didn't play again until a divisional trial, where I played badly and it resulted in me not representing my country.

A safe scrum

Players in the front row of the scrum can suffer neck, back, shoulder and head injuries. To prevent this, players in the front row of the scrum must never twist their bodies or do anything that may collapse the scrum, as this could result in serious injury. The back row must also remain bound properly until the scrum has ended.

The scrum can be a dangerous place if players do not abide by the rules.

Matches

During the season, academy players play at least one game a week. All the players' training and preparation are put to the test during a match.

Match preparation

Players need to warm up and stretch their muscles before a match to reduce the chance of injury. The warm-up will also increase the body's temperature and blood flow to allow players to perform at their best.

Preparations for a match are mental as well as physical. Self belief can be an important factor in a good performance. The coach and team captain talk to the players before a match and motivate them to perform as well as they can.

Before a match we have meetings to discuss tactics. We watch the opposing team in video analysis sessions and pick out the weak points in attack and defence. As a fly half, you have to be very cool-headed and be able to make clinical decisions. The motto is: 'Body on fire, head in the fridge.'

There are a lot of stretches that we do before a game. All of them involve stretching the whole body from head to toe. I usually concentrate on leg swings as they relate to kicking well. I have a private routine that I go through in my head to get me focused before a match. Normally everyone is quiet for a while, concentrating on the game, but then we usually have a team talk to make sure everyone knows the patterns and to make sure everyone is ready to do battle.

It takes stamina to perform at a high level for the full 80 minutes of a rugby union match.

Scoring a try is worth five points in a match. A try is scored when players touch the ball on the ground in their opponents' goal area.

Match rules

Rugby has a lot of rules to remember and follow. The referee is assisted by touch judges. Sometimes a video referee is in charge of the game. The video referee watches footage of the game and makes the final decision on points, for example, on whether a try is awarded. However physical the game is getting, it is the captain's responsibility to keep all the players under control. Individuals who break the rules risk being sent off the pitch to the '**sin bin**' for ten minutes, so their team is a player short, or be given a red card and sent off for the rest of the game.

Cool down

After a match players need to relax their muscles and bring their heart rate back to normal. They do this by doing a series of stretches. This also breaks down the waste products in the muscles that are created by strenuous exercise.

Sometimes players sit in a bath full of ice after a game. This can be a shock to the system at first, but it is a good way of reducing swelling and cooling down the muscles.

Analyse and improve

Every player experiences bad games as well as good ones. The secret is to learn from every performance to build experience and improve as a player.

Coach's notes: matches

The work you do in between matches is the key to improving performance.

Matches are opportunities to demonstrate skills, and learn what else you need to work on to improve your game.

Sporting heroes

Carlos Spencer (left) of Northampton passes the ball during a match between Saracens and Northampton Saints in 2008.

Top-level rugby players are heroes for the many fans of the sport. They are an inspiration to youngsters starting out in the sport, and their conduct on and off the pitch sets an example for others to follow.

Carlos Spencer
Fly half
(New Zealand All Blacks, Auckland Blues and Northampton Saints)

Carlos Spencer scored 33 points in his first test for the New Zealand All Blacks in 1995. He played in the All Blacks World Cup squad in 2003.

My first rugby hero, probably like most fly halves and rugby players, was Jonny Wilkinson; I admired him for his playing ability and his precision kicking. Then as I developed as a player, I started to look up to more flair players, the likes of Carlos Spencer and Dan Carter of New Zealand. I like the way in which all three of these players will play on the edge and try to make something out of nothing, but they will always do their basic jobs well. I try and copy Wilkinson's kicking ability, Carter's distribution and running ability and Spencer's flair.

Jonny Wilkinson OBE
Fly half
(England, Newcastle Falcons)

Jonny Wilkinson is most famous for scoring the winning drop goal in the last minute of extra time against Australia in the Rugby World Cup final in 2003. He is the highest points scorer in Rugby World Cup history.

My first rugby hero was Jonny Wilkinson, as I first started playing at around the time of the 2003 Rugby World Cup. Now I look up to players such as Richard Hill, who have accomplished everything in the game. He has won the World Cup with England, played in Lions tests and been at the top of the Premiership game for over a decade. He is a true legend. My hero is now my mentor at the club. Richard Hill is there to go through any issues I have on and off the field. It is a great honour to have his services to such a personal degree. I am trying to adopt his toughness and aggression around the field.

Jonny Wilkinson (left) and Richard Hill of England celebrate after England's victory in the 2003 Rugby World Cup Final match between Australia and England.

Richard Hill MBE
Flanker
(England, Saracens)

Richard Hill is a former rugby union footballer who played flanker for Saracens and England. He retired in 2008. He was part of the victorious England squad in the 2003 Rugby Union World Cup.

The next step

Making a career as a professional rugby player requires dedication as well as skill and talent. Some players continue to play at the highest level into their thirties, but rugby is a hard physical sport and injuries are very common. Players often continue in the sport as coaches after their playing career is over, passing on their expertise to a new generation of players.

Plans and ambitions

Jackson, Jake, Sam and Jamie are all hoping to be offered professional contracts to play for Saracens when they reach 18.

Coach's notes: plans

Dedication, talent and mental strength are key to career success, but all players, no matter how good, have to have contingency or fall-back plans. No one is immune to injury in a game like rugby.

My ultimate ambition would be to play international rugby, but my next target is to make England under-18s Six Nations squad. In five years' time I would love to be playing in the Premiership for Saracens.

My ambition is to eventually work myself into the Saracens first team and earn a starting place. My next target on the way to that is to play well in the next A team games in order to be worthy of a place in the first team. I must use my training between now and then to prepare myself mentally and physically. In five years' time I could see myself hopefully being in the first team starting position. As a 23-year-old, I would hope to be involved regularly in and around the first team.

My ultimate ambition is to be a professional rugby player and my next target on the way to achieving that is to make the England under-18s team.

They are aiming to play rugby in the Premiership. Some players, such as Jackson and Jake, plan to combine their studies with their professional rugby career.

International competitions

For all sportsmen and women there is something very special about representing your country in international competitions. In rugby union there are three major international competitions. The Rugby World Cup takes place every four years and is played between national teams from all over the world. The Six Nations tournament takes place every year and is between England, France, Ireland, Italy, Scotland and Wales. The Tri Nations competition is also held every year and is between Australia, New Zealand and South Africa.

My ultimate ambition is to get a professional contract and play in the Premiership for Saracens and represent England to gain a full cap. The next target is to keep competing at the highest level possible at Saracens, and to represent England under-18s in the Six Nations. To get to my next target, I will need to train hard and eat right and make the right decisions. Within the next five years, I would like to have graduated from university, be a regular in the Saracens first team and to be pushing for an England shirt.

If you play rugby at the top level there is a fair bit of money to be made, but I'm not in the game for the money. I am in it for the love of the sport.

Sam, Jamie, Jackson and Jake are all well on the way to a career in professional rugby. Let's wish them luck for the future.

Glossary

adrenaline A hormone that is released into the bloodstream in response to physical or mental stress. It stimulates the body to perform at its maximum level.

back One of the positions from 9 to 15 in a rugby union team.

campus The grounds and buildings of a college, university or school.

caps Players win caps when they are selected for a national squad.

cardiovascular Involving the heart and blood vessels.

centre Positions 12 and 13 in a rugby union team.

concussion Injury to the brain caused by the impact of a collision.

conversion A kick at goal awarded after a try has been scored. A successful conversion is worth two points.

drop goal A goal scored from a drop kick.

drop kick Dropping the ball and kicking it as it begins to rise after touching the ground.

dummies Moves designed to make your opponent believe you are actually about to make the pass, while at the last moment you do not let go of the ball.

flankers The players in the back row of the forwards on the far right and far left of the pack.

fly half Position 10 in a rugby union team. A fly half organises the attack and defence.

hand-eye co-ordination The ability to see and control the ball.

infringement The breaking of a rule.

lactic acid A substance produced in the muscles during exercise. Too much lactic acid can cause cramping pains.

lateral To the side.

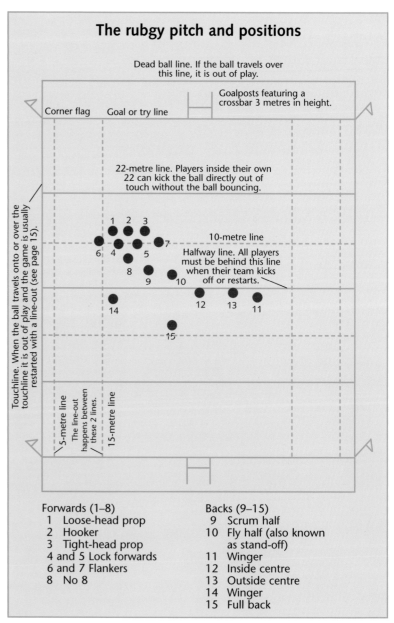

The rubgy pitch and positions

Dead ball line. If the ball travels over this line, it is out of play.

Goalposts featuring a crossbar 3 metres in height.

Corner flag   Goal or try line

22-metre line. Players inside their own 22 can kick the ball directly out of touch without the ball bouncing.

10-metre line

Halfway line. All players must be behind this line when their team kicks off or restarts.

Touchline. When the ball travels onto or over the touchline it is out of play and the game is usually restarted with a line-out (see page 15).

5-metre line

The line-out happens between these 2 lines.

15-metre line

Forwards (1–8)
1 Loose-head prop
2 Hooker
3 Tight-head prop
4 and 5 Lock forwards
6 and 7 Flankers
8 No 8

Backs (9–15)
 9 Scrum half
10 Fly half (also known as stand-off)
11 Winger
12 Inside centre
13 Outside centre
14 Winger
15 Full back

line-out A way of restarting play after the ball has been knocked or kicked out of play past the touch line.

nutrition The scientific study of food and drink.

pack The forwards in a rugby union team.

penalty A kick awarded to the opposing team if a rule is broken.

place kick A kick made when the ball is placed on a kicking tee or into a hole in the pitch made by a player's heel.

possession When your team has control of the ball.

pre-season Just before the main playing season starts.

prop Two players on the right and left of the front row forwards. The props play an important part in the scrum.

scrum A way of re-starting play after a minor infringement, such as passing or knocking a ball forward.

scrum half A back in position nine who plays the ball between the forwards and the backs.

sidesteps Sideways moves made to avoid being tackled.

sin bin The bench where all players who have committed a yellow card offence sit out of the game for ten minutes.

swerves Ways of moving to avoid being tackled.

tackle To bring a player who is carrying the ball to the ground.

try A way of scoring points in a match by touching the ball on the ground inside the opposition's goal area.

Find out more

Websites

www.talkrugbyunion.co.uk
A lot of really useful information about all aspects of rugby union.

www.rugbyunionrules.com
A very clear site that explains the rules of rugby union.

www.rugbytactics.com/animated/ drills.php
A rugby tactics site that uses simple animation to explain different rugby moves and drills.

Book

Know Your Sport: Rugby – Clive Gifford (Franklin Watts, 2006)
A guide to rugby, with step-by-step photographs as well as profiles and statistics giving information about some of the world's greatest rugby players.

Index